Derry in Old Photographs

Derry in Old Photographs

Art Byrne and Sean McMahon

GILL & MACMILLAN

Gill & Macmillan Ltd
Hume Avenue
Park West
Dublin 12
with associated companies throughout the world
www.gillmacmillan.ie

© 2003 Art Byrne and Sean McMahon
0 7171 3641 8

Design and print origination by O'K Graphic Design, Dublin
Printed in Malaysia

*The paper used in this book is made from the wood pulp of managed forests.
For every tree felled, at least one tree is planted, thereby renewing natural resources.*

A catalogue record is available for this book from the British Library.

1 3 5 4 2

Contents

INTRODUCTION   vi

ACKNOWLEDGMENTS   ix

1. LOVELY DERRY ON THE BANKS OF THE FOYLE   1

2. CREEPING LIKE SNAIL . . .   13

3. ETERNAL VERITIES   21

4. THAT'S ENTERTAINMENT   35

5. HIGH DAYS   47

6. EARNING THEIR BREAD   57

7. PLAYING THE GAME   74

8. TRAINS AND BOATS AND PLANES   84

9. POLLS APART   96

10. WARS AND RUMOURS OF WAR   105

place, and the local impact of the Second World War that shook the place out of its depressed somnolence is also preserved on glass and celluloid.

The darker side of Derry life — its poverty, its rancid politics, its community divisions — cannot be ignored, but the natural tendency of all Irish people, whatever their attitudes, towards craic cannot long be dammed. There were dances, mannequin parades, Sunday school outings, regattas and feiseanna, and the camera eye indiscriminately caught and stored them for later generations. The impression that all these photographs give of the city may be as flickering and shadowy as an old silent film, but perhaps with patience the interested viewer will be able to devise a composite picture of what, to its chauvinistic inhabitants, is still 'lovely Derry on the banks of the Foyle'.

Acknowledgments

We would like to take this opportunity to thank Lewis Childs, Joseph McLaughlin and Stephanie McMullan of the library of the University of Ulster; Bernadette Walsh of the Harbour Museum of the Derry City Council; Dick Sinclair of the Central Library, Derry; Dermot Carlin of St Columb's College; John McCandless of the Nerve Centre; Bernadette Barr, Sean Crawford, Richard Doherty, Pat McCafferty, Anna McMahon, Wendy Mackey, Eddie Mailey — and primarily David Bigger, whose book essentially this is.

Art Byrne and Sean McMahon

1
Lovely Derry on the Banks of the Foyle

T his section might equally have been titled 'Out and About in the Maiden City'. It is meant to give a general overview of what the place looked like (and indeed still largely does in spite of changes that older denizens might regard as seismic). Derry, more than most Irish towns, is defined by its topography. The river is wide (and, of course, beautiful) and over the centuries of the city's formal existence the problem of getting from the west to the east bank has had to be dealt with. The encroachment into Donegal — Inishowen to be precise, at the time of the seventeenth-century grant to the Honourable, the Irish Society — was partly to give more territory to the London companies, but also to help defend the walled city that lay entirely on the Foyle's left bank. This meant that a deep and often swift-flowing river had to be crossed to reach County Londonderry and the civility of the planted lands, well away from the wrath of the dispossessed. Eventually bridges were built, the earliest greatly helped by one of Derry's sterling benefactors, the Earl Bishop. The memory of that time persists in such addresses as Ferryquay Street, Bridge Street (though it ceased to run to the bridge in 1863) and, of course, Ferryquay Gate which was the one the London apprentices shut in December 1688 and started the famous siege. The walls still stand and though the gates are now rarely closed, they still mark the boundary-outlets for the well-designed town that played an extraordinary part in the War of the Three Kings. Shipquay Street, Shipquay Place and Shipquay Gate hint at a different story, of commerce, emigration and the darker days of war. It is also appropriate that this general picture of the city should have photographs of walls, gates, bridges and public transport (at a time when private cars were a genuine luxury) to help its pedestrian population survive in what the Meath poet Francis Ledwidge, stationed there briefly in 1916, called 'Derry of the little hills'.

One of the earliest photographs of Derry taken *c.1872*. It was for use with a stereoscope. The instrument had eye-pieces like binoculars and the images, taken at slightly different angles, were viewed concurrently, one with each eye, creating a three-dimensional effect. The pictures show Magee College that had been inaugurated on Tuesday, 10 October 1865, and the Foyle.

A view of Bishop Gate, taken for a book on the siege of Derry. It was at this gate that James II appeared on 18 April 1689 in pouring rain, to be met with the famous cry of 'No surrender!'

Sir Percy Walter Greenaway, Lord Mayor of London, at the opening of Craigavon Bridge in March 1933. The bridge was a two-tier construction, the lower deck intended for rail traffic so that the four termini NCC, CDR, GNR and L&LS were linked. The choice of name, that of the first prime minister of Northern Ireland, was unpopular with the majority nationalist population of the city.

Sir Percy Walter Greenaway's coach, at the opening of the new bridge, March 1933. (Harbour Museum; Derry City Council)

Strand Road in the mid-1920s, showing Sawers shop at the corner of Sackville Street where the Bank of Ireland (formerly the National Bank) now stands. The milk cart was characteristic of pre-hygienic times and the bus was operated by the Municipal Omnibus Service. The Municipal Technical College (1908) can be seen on the extreme right of the picture. (Bigger-McDonald Collection)

Bridge Street leading from Ferryquay Gate to Foyle Street c.1940. It took its name from the old wooden bridge which crossed the river. It, like most of Foyle Street, has been entirely rebuilt. (Bigger-McDonald Collection)

Postcard view of Shipquay Place c.1890. It shows the cars of the City of Derry Tramway Company owned by McFarland which plied between Carlisle Square and the Londonderry & Lough Swilly Railway Station for a fare of one old penny. At each terminus the horses were unhitched and led round to the other end of the car. (Richard Doherty)

Shipquay Place from a 1930s postcard. A Catherwood bus is making its way towards the Strand. Catherwoods were finally bought out by the semi-state Northern Ireland Road Transport Board (NIRTB), which became the Ulster Transport Authority (UTA) in 1947 when transport was nationalised. (Richard Doherty)

Ferryquay Gate *c.*1926 from Carlisle Road and with Ferryquay Street seen through the central arch. It was the site of one of the four original gates of the walled city, the one that was shut by the London Apprentice Boys on 7 December 1688, thus precipitating the famous siege. The gate, then known as New Gate, was closed against the Earl of Antrim's Jacobite soldiers who had crossed to the ferry quay at the foot of the hill. The pedestrian arches and indeed all the facings are modern, designed by Robert Collins in 1866. (University of Ulster)

The Casino and grounds in Bishop Street, site of St Columb's College from November 1879. Though more than adequately housed in his episcopal palace in Bishop Street Within, Frederick Hervey (1730–1803), the eccentric Earl Bishop, decided he needed a summer house (the meaning of 'casino' in those days) and built it in diocesan grounds, a mere half-mile from his official residence. The site had become a private park until the building of the college began in 1877. (St Columb's College)

The city wall *c.*1930 above Shipquay Place showing the Northern Bank and the now vanished Northern Counties Hotel. The cannons, relics of the siege, have since been refurbished. (University of Ulster)

Carlisle Road, looking up towards Ferryquay Gate *c.*1930. (Bigger-McDonald Collection)

Ferryquay Street in the mid-1930s, showing the recently opened Woolworth's and the man with the label 'Blind from Birth' whose permanent pitch it was. (Bigger-McDonald Collection)

An ice ship. In the days before universal refrigeration, ice was regularly brought to Derry from Norway and Greenland. The practice is remembered in the name of a new bar called the Ice Wharf, close to the original dock. (Bigger-McDonald Collection)

Where town met country, as Creggan Road became truly rural. The railings beyond the last house belonged to the Rosemount Girls' Public Elementary School. (Richard Doherty)

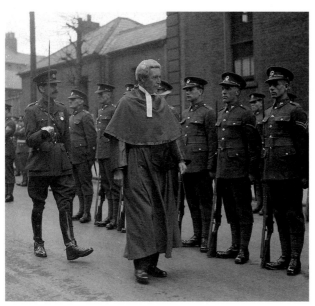

A judge inspecting a guard of honour at the Winter Assizes outside the episcopal palace (the Masonic Hall since 1945). The original building was largely reconstructed by the Earl Bishop in 1770. During the 1798 Rising it was used to house soldiers. (Bigger-McDonald Collection)

Duke Street, now largely demolished and rebuilt, in sunshine and shadow. It was here on 5 October 1968 that the attack by the RUC on the Civil Rights marchers occurred, an event regarded by many as the true beginning of the Northern Troubles. (Bigger-McDonald Collection)

When St Columb's College was opened in November 1879 as a diocesan seminary, the Earl Bishop's Casino was adapted as the college chapel. These pupils of the 1880s seem quite relaxed in front of its Ionian façade. (St Columb's College)

A second-hand clothes shop seen through Butcher Gate during the First World War. The policeman on duty, an RIC constable, is deliberately not looking at the open cellar doors of John McMonagle's public house. The torn notices on the gate reflect war nerves concerning the restriction of aliens. (Charles Logue)

2
Creeping like Snail . . .

Life for children in Derry over the period when these pictures were taken was as pleasant (or unpleasant) as in any other Irish town. School was no more attractive to those with shining morning faces than it was in Shakespeare's day. They faced reading and writing and 'rithmetic, in those days taught 'to the tune of the hickory stick' (as the old song put it), or hickory's bamboo or leather equivalents. Life, however, wasn't all seven-times tables, spellings or Vere Foster headlines, warning the steel pen-pushers that 'Habits can gain a Samson's strength' or 'Least said, soonest mended.' When the bell rang for lunchtime, or better still, home-time, the young philosophers found more interesting uses for their ink-stained fingers than copying barely understood proverbs. Homework was a distant cloud and the morning's class an unlikely nightmare. The town had its parks and safe, almost traffic-free streets for all the seasonal games: marbles, spinning tops, skipping and swinging round lampposts. The carriageway on the walls that ringed the older city made a splendid playground. Later some would move to secondary schools to learn the secrets of the Bunsen burner or the best way to achieve perspective in primitive architectural drawing. College boys and girls who played serious games like rugby and hockey were not really envied and at the beginning of the period their uniforms were rather more rudimentary than the later conformity of scarf and blazer. The city had its own third-level establishment, an expression not in use then, in Magee College. It was opened in 1865 as a Presbyterian seminary, but by 1909 it had a considerable number of non-divinity students, both men and women. In its understated way the city was able to care for the educational needs of its children from their earliest days. Elderly praisers of the past tend to view even schooldays in a golden light, but the details of the level of competence in academic subjects required then for the Primary Leaving Certificate examination are enough to make the average Leaving Certificate student blanch.

A photograph of a baby taken by Harry Craig, chemist of Ferryquay Street, *c.*1930. (Bigger-McDonald Collection)

Master Edwards in a sailor suit posed against an appropriate stormy seascape. (Bigger-McDonald Collection)

Unidentified schoolboy *c*.1910. (St Columb's College)

Children posing on a Crimean War cannon in front of Gwyn's Institution. The building was erected in 1840 to Thomas Jackson's design with money from the legacy of John Gwyn, a prosperous grocer, as an orphanage for boys. The legend has it that he had asked several girls to run an errand for him but was refused. The son of a widowed mother finally obliged and he never forgot it. Another philanthropist, James Young, supplied the money to have the charity extended to girls. By 1900 the building served as the City Museum and Municipal Library. (Bigger-McDonald Collection)

Children being escorted across Northland Road from the Model School gate in 1932. (Bigger-McDonald Collection)

The science laboratory in the Christian Brothers' School *c*.1912. (Bigger-McDonald Collection)

St Columb's College some time before 1895. It shows the first building opened on 3 November 1879, and later known as Junior House, and the original Casino building which served as the college chapel. (St Columb's College)

Pupils of St Columb's some time after 1881 when the double ball court was built. (St Columb's College)

Staff and students of Magee College *c.*1937. From 1909 Magee students took the final two years of their degrees in Trinity College, Dublin. This association with Trinity was to cause some logistical problems over financing after 1920. It also meant an increase in the number of non-divinity students. The connection with Trinity, however, continued until the opening of the New University of Ulster in 1970. (Bigger-McDonald Collection)

Boys playing marbles at the church wall beside the cathedral railings. (Bigger-McDonald Collection)

Miss McCrea, the sister of Basil McCrea, a trustee of Magee College, who provided £7,000 to finance a chair of Natural Philosophy in 1905 and later left £70,000 to the college, subject to her life interest. In 1911 she gave a further £5,000 and in December of that year, in recognition of that generosity, the name of the college was changed to McCrea-Magee Presbyterian College, Londonderry. (University of Ulster)

Children from Londonderry High School kindergarten at painting class in the art room. (Bigger-McDonald Collection)

3
Eternal Verities

I n the Derry of the period covered by this book religion, that divinely divisive entity, played its all-embracing part. The usual priestly duties, succinctly if crudely described as hatching, matching and dispatching, were carried out and the pictorial evidence remains. Funerals were recorded in newspapers only if the deceased were people of significance, by small city standards. When Bishop O'Kane's body was brought to Derry on 6 January 1939 from Kilrea, Co. Derry, where he had died, so many people met the cortège at the city's edge that traffic stopped and the police had to deal with the uncharacteristic disruption. People got married in church, chapel, meeting-house and synagogue, and these places of worship needed maintenance. Bells had to be recast, roofs made secure. As the population grew new buildings were needed, and some elegant edifices became part of the city's architectural store. The various sects in the city lived religiously exclusive lives, maintaining a distant respect for separated brethren, and worshipping in their time-honoured way. Sometimes a seasonal festivity brought greater fervour. In the Long Tower parish, dedicated to Colum Cille, the patron of the city, his feast day, 9 June, saw children and adults alike with oak leaves in their lapels honouring the saint who was believed to have said that the oaks of his beloved Doire Choluim Chille were filled with angels. (The decorating of houses with ragwort on May Day was tributary to a much older belief.) In June 1932 the city responded to the thirty-first Eucharistic Congress that brought a million people to open-air Mass in the Phoenix Park, Dublin. Decorative arches adorned Catholic parts of the city and houses were decorated with the Congress icon, a purple Greek cross, traces of which could be seen on walls for years after. The cross became the centrepiece of the rose window of the new St Patrick's Church, Pennyburn, the foundation stone of which had been laid in Congress year. A number of babies were christened Pascal in 1932 in commemoration of the Congress.

A crowd gathered around the holy well in St Columb's Wells on the saint's feast day, 9 June c.1945. (Bigger-McDonald Collection)

The bells of St Columb's Cathedral were taken down for refurbishment *c*.1930. (Bigger-McDonald Collection)

The arrival of the refurbished bell at Derry Quay *c*.1930. (Bigger-McDonald Collection)

The wedding of Diana Watchman of Derry and Sydney Shaw of Glasgow at the Jewish synagogue in Kennedy Place in August 1939. (Bigger-McDonald Collection)

A wedding at Gt James's Street Presbyterian Church in the 1920s. The church was built in 1835–37 to the design of Stewart Gordon as the Third Derry Presbyterian, though it was also known as the Scots church. Owing to a shift in population because of the Troubles, it ceased to be used as a church in the mid-1970s. It served for a time as the city library and later as a glass factory. (Bigger-McDonald Collection)

A wedding party leaving Ebrington Presbyterian Church, Limavady Road, in the 1920s. The church, built in 1897, has a temple front and Corinthian columns. The architect was William Barker. (Bigger-McDonald Collection)

Methodist service in the People's Hall, Barrack Street, in the early stages of its construction. (Bigger-McDonald Collection)

The People's Hall, Barrack Street, not long after it opened. It was used as a Methodist hall and as a night refuge. It was demolished for redevelopment with the rest of the houses in the street in the 1980s. (Bigger-McDonald Collection)

Francis Kelly (1812–89), the Catholic Bishop of Derry, builder of St Eugene's Cathedral (1873) and St Columb's College (1879). He was born in Drumragh in 1812 and appointed as Coadjutor Bishop of Derry in 1849. He inherited a diocese ravaged by famine and depressed by poverty, but in the forty years of his episcopate he built confidence in his people and made available some form of education for them. He left as his memorial a fine cathedral and a diocesan seminary. (St Columb's College)

Bishop Bernard O'Kane (1867–1939) presenting Fr John McConalogue (1842–1933), the parish priest of Aghyaran, with a memorial book on the occasion of his diamond jubilee as a priest in 1931. A political activist, McConalogue was a friend of Michael Davitt (1846–1906), the founder of the Land League, who stayed with him when he visited West Tyrone. (Bigger-McDonald Collection)

Portrait and subject. (St Columb's College)

The president of St Columb's College, Rev. Joseph O'Doherty (1895–1978), prior to the unveiling of a portrait of the previous president, Bishop Neil Farren (1893–1980). Bishop Farren was born in Buncrana and after his ordination served on the staff of St Columb's College (1927–39). He was consecrated bishop on 1 October 1939 in St Eugene's Cathedral. His long episcopate saw the Second World War, the post-war social changes and the darkest days of the Northern Troubles. (St Columb's College)

A welcoming party at the city boundary to greet Cardinal MacRory on 1 October 1939 on his visit to consecrate Fr Neil Farren as Bishop of Derry. The party includes Frank McCarroll, Laurence Duffy, Jack Towers and Fr James Bonner, administrator of St Eugene's Cathedral. (Bigger-McDonald Collection)

Bishop Farren leaving the GNR station on the 1952 diocesan pilgrimage to Lourdes. In the days before universal air travel the larger part of the journey was overland in special trains. (Bigger-McDonald Collection)

Bishop Bernard O'Kane laying the foundation stone of St Patrick's Church, Pennyburn, on 23 February 1932. The church, designed by E. J. Toye, is of red brick with sandstone facings and a large wheel window. It was completed two years later and dedicated by the bishop on 27 May 1934 — the first twentieth-century church to be built in the city. (Bigger-McDonald Collection)

A procession to St Columb's Cathedral on the occasion of the 300th anniversary of the founding in 1633. The builder was William Parrott who made a contract with the Honourable, the Irish Society, in 1628 to provide a suitable church for the new city. The Earl Bishop added a spire in 1776 which had to be taken down in 1802 because it proved too heavy for the tower. Its present-day replacement dates from 1822. (Bigger-McDonald Collection)

A Corpus Christi procession in the late 1930s. (Bigger-McDonald Collection)

A Corpus Christi procession *c.*1930 in the grounds of St Columb's College. (St Columb's College)

A memorial arch in Rossville Street celebrating the Eucharistic Congress. The Congress (for the promotion of devotion to the Blessed Sacrament) was held in Dublin on 22–6 June 1932. Its high point was the celebration of High Mass in the Phoenix Park, Dublin, before an audience of a million people. There were other celebrations countrywide, with many houses decorated with the Congress icon, an adapted Celtic cross.

A procession of Nazareth House children at the funeral of Mgr Philip O'Doherty (1851–1927), Bishop Street, in February 1927. Mgr O'Doherty was very active in nationalist politics. He was involved with the Land League and was a strong supporter of Justin McCarthy MP (1830–1912) in the successful 1886 election. He is buried under a large Celtic cross in the graveyard of the Long Tower Church. (St Columb's College)

The funeral of a fireman on a winter's day in Spencer Road, passing Simpson's Brae on its way to Glendermot Cemetery c.1930. (Bigger-McDonald Collection)

The remains of Bishop O'Kane being carried into St Eugene's Cathedral on 6 January 1939. Bernard O'Kane was born in Garvagh in 1867 and became one of the earliest and brightest of the students in the new junior seminary of St Columb's (1879), winning a gold medal for taking first place in Ireland in the Intermediate Examination in 1882. He was president of his old school, 1905–19, and consecrated bishop in 1926. He published many papers in radio telegraphy, rivalling Marconi in his research. (St Columb's College)

The Towers brothers as chief mourners at a family funeral c.1933. The family owned the wholesale grocery firm of O'Neill & McHenry. (Bigger-McDonald Collection)

Fire officer Trimble's funeral in St Columb's Court on the way to the cathedral *c.*1935. (Bigger-McDonald Collection)

4
That's Entertainment

I n the 1930s there were seven cinemas in Derry: the Strand, City, Palace, Rialto, St Columb's Hall, Midland and the Opera House, two feiseanna, many dance halls and innumerable pubs. To the DVD generation, when even traditional VCRs seem old hat and television is as familiar as wallpaper, the idea of a life where radio (or the wireless as it was called then) was the only touch-of-the-switch entertainment is impossible to imagine. Olden days, indeed, to use the favourite phrase of the young. The 'talkies' came in 1928 and the cinema queues never lessened until the 1960s. The Opera House staged many a live show, both professional and amateur, and tended towards cine-variety with the emphasis as the years went by on the 'cine'. It burned down in a freak fire in 1940 and Derry lost its only purpose-built theatre. It had been a popular venue with cross-channel professional companies. They did their week, playing the last house on a Saturday night, and knew that the *Lairdsloch* or some other 'Scotch boat' would wait for them at the quay and have them on the Broomilaw Quay in Glasgow on the Sunday. There were, however, other venues for concerts, plays and soirées. The city's deserved and well-maintained reputation for musicality was the product of much work and dedication. There was music in the Derry air, as its harmonious laureate has written. Dance bands swung, as did the dancers at céilí and old times; singers crooned; and choirs, mixed-voice and single-gender, harmonised the sweetest music this side of heaven. People did not sit in shaded rooms staring at small screens but got out more. Pantomimes, operettas and ambitious school shows were responsible for the fact that the people in the streets knew most of the Gilbert and Sullivan operas, and most Irish operas, and could outcall Rose Marie. In spite of slump, economic starvation and overlong dole queues, there *was* entertainment.

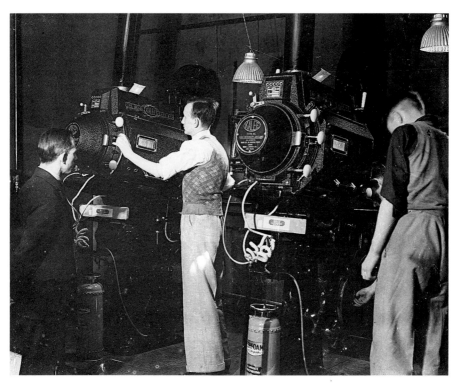

The projection room in the Strand Cinema, the last (and sole surviving) cinema to be opened in Derry. A Curran cinema, its 1,600-seat auditorium first admitted spectators on Christmas Eve 1934 and, appropriate to the golden age of cinema, it also had a café which closed at the end of the 1950s. The picture shows, on the left, Freddie Box, the chief projectionist, checking the equipment. (Bigger-McDonald Collection)

The exterior of the Palace Cinema *c.*1930 during refurbishment, which included a new sound system for 'talkies' and a new balcony. (Bigger-McDonald Collection)

The City in William Street, the first purpose-built cinema in Derry. It became the chief source of Saturday matinées for children in the 1930s and 40s. The stall seats cost two old pennies, while the balcony was one penny dearer. The afternoon programme closed with an episode from a serial which always ended in suspense. Known to the clients as the 'continuous', the serials featured Flash Gordon, the Lone Ranger, and a recurring favourite called *The Clutching Hand*. (Bigger-McDonald Collection)

Children, one wearing the uniform of the Londonderry High School, skating along a traffic-free Limavady Road in the 1930s. (Bigger-McDonald Collection)

A visit of the Naturalists' Field Club to St Columb's College in 1936. The visitors led by Fred Logan are being conveyed by the president of the college, Rev. Neil Farren. Their particular object of interest was the seventeenth-century windmill tower in the college grounds. (Bigger-McDonald Collection)

A realistic car crash from some play, probably in the Opera House to judge by the effectiveness of the stage props. The theatre was opened in 1877 as the Royal Opera House by J. F. Warden and became a cine-variety theatre in the 1930s. Warden was born in Hull in 1836 and learned his trade as a travelling actor. The theatre was sold to H. B. Phillips (1866–1950), a local music dealer and entrepreneur, in 1896. (Bigger-McDonald Collection)

Nymphs of spring in St Columb's Park in the 1930s. (Bigger-McDonald Collection)

A scene from Sigmund Romberg's *The Desert Song* (1926) in the Opera House. When the theatre began to show films its elaborate interior was covered with a plain plasterboard façade as more appropriate to a cinema. One night in 1940 a small fire was started accidentally, backstage. The whole place was alight within a matter of seconds and the theatre was gutted. (Bigger-McDonald Collection)

The cast of a children's play in Wesley Hall, Carlisle Road. (Bigger-McDonald Collection)

A group of Irish dancers on the quays behind the Guildhall during Easter week. (Bigger-McDonald Collection)

St Columb's College pupils' orchestra *c.*1927, with the president, Dr John McShane (1877–1956), and the conductor, J. O'Brien. (St Columb's College)

An unidentified prize-winning choir *c.*1920. (Pat McCafferty)

The Kerry Blue class in a dog show held *c.*1927 in Victoria Market, Strand Road. (Bigger-McDonald Collection)

The Aileach Choir with Leo Hutton as conductor, winners of the McDonald cup for the third consecutive year. The choir under Hutton had taken part in a successful prize-winners' concert in 1927, the first to be broadcast from the city, which was relayed to the station in Belfast. (Pat McCafferty)

The Feis Doire Colmcille committee. The feis was launched on 27 June 1922 with 700 entries and ran for four days, Tuesday to Friday. This picture shows the committee and adjudicators for 1923, including Fr John Logue McGettigan (1868–1946), one of the prime movers in setting up the feis, and Dr John F. Larchet (1884–1967), the chief music adjudicator. (Pat McCafferty)

Mannequins in Austin's department store 1932. (Bigger-McDonald Collection)

A photograph showing John McCabe and the winning men's choir in the 1940s, taken outside the parochial house, St Eugene's Cathedral. John McCabe, a teacher, was an important figure in the musical life of a self-consciously musical city. (Courtesy Pat McCafferty)

The cast of an unidentified school entertainment in St Columb's College in the 1920s outside the original building which was opened in 1879. To judge by the historical range of the costumes and the variety of characters, it may well have been a pageant rather than a drama.

A party of sightseers in the graveyard of St Columb's Cathedral led by the mayor, Sir James Wilton (1934). (Bigger-McDonald Collection)

James McCafferty and a mixed-voice choir, 1950. James McCafferty, who was born in 1915, spent most of his life as a professional musician: singer, pianist, accompanist, orchestra leader, dance band conductor, choirmaster and teacher. One of the most significant figures in Derry's musical life, he died in 1995. (Pat McCafferty)

An unknown lady harpist c.1880s. (Bigger-McDonald Collection)

5
High Days

erry and the City of London, the postal district that used to be known as EC1, share an unlikely distinction: each has a Guildhall. (They also share officially the name London, but that's a controversy too heated for rational discourse.) James I decided that the only means of bringing civility to wild Ulster was to plant it with willing leal men. (Nowadays we would call them loyalists.) He dismissed the working County of Coleraine and created County Londonderry, added the prefix London to the north-west city and imposed responsibility for city and county on the very reluctant London guilds. On 29 March 1635 the Charter of Londonderry was impressed by the royal seal and the city began its modern career. It was in honour of the London connection that when a new town hall was built in 1890 to replace the one that had previously stood in the Diamond, it was to be known as the Guildhall. It was built on reclaimed land at the foot of Shipquay Street and it lasted for eighteen years. There was great excitement when the foundation stone was laid, and even greater dismay when, on Easter Sunday, 19 April 1908, the elaborately designed building caught fire and was effectively razed to the ground. Lack of an adequate water supply and an undermanned fire service were blamed for its complete destruction. One enterprising local photographer added very realistic flames to a picture of the shell and made a nice profit on the postcard. Fire and flood remained the likely sources of off-stage urban drama but the city, depressed from its economic blow when through Partition it lost its hinterland, had another high day when Amelia Earhart, the intrepid aviatrix (as the few women pilots were called in those decorous days), landed her plane in a field north of the city on 21 May 1932.

Lower William Street during one of the regular floods that accompanied heavy rain. In 1937 a new drainage system was introduced and the risk of flooding receded. (Bigger-McDonald Collection)

The announcement at the Council Hall in the Diamond of the accession of Edward VII (1841–1910). Queen Victoria died at her house at Osborne on the Isle of Wight at 6.30 p.m. on 22 January 1901 in her eighty-second year. The tidings of the beginning of the new reign were proclaimed the next day. (Central Library, Derry)

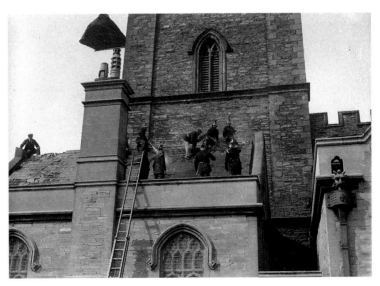

Firemen on the roof of the chapter house of St Columb's Cathedral after the fire of 1935. (Bigger-McDonald Collection)

Fire in the chapter house of St Columb's Cathedral on 15 May 1935 caused by an electrical fault. The Duke of Gloucester (1900–1974), the third son of George V, was due to visit that day. (Bigger-McDonald Collection)

The burnt-out shell of Derry's Guildhall. It was destroyed in a fire on Easter Sunday, 19 April 1908, and contemporary blame was placed firmly on the councillors for their neglect of the fire service and failure to provide an adequate water supply. Reconstruction began almost immediately and the building, now with more elaborate tracery, was opened again in 1913. (University of Ulster)

Laying the foundations of the Guildhall in 1887. The building was designed by John Guy Ferguson and opened in 1890. Its four-faced clock and regular chimes are still an important part of the city's atmosphere. It replaced the Market House, the former town hall, which was sited in the Diamond. The name was a piece of polite flattery to the Irish Society in London, which had been given the task of founding the modern city in 1610. (Harbour Museum; Derry City Council)

The ruins of the Guildhall after the 1908 fire, seen from inside. (Harbour Museum; Derry City Council)

The steel skeleton of the clock tower of the Guildhall, 1910, as it was being rebuilt after the fire. (Harbour Museum; Derry City Council)

Amelia Earhart (1897–1937) and her plane, *Friendship*, a Lockheed Vega, in a field at Springfield, Ballyarnett, where she made an emergency landing at 1.30 p.m. on 21 May 1932. She was the first woman to fly the Atlantic solo and her intended terminus was Paris. She had hoped to emulate Lindbergh's solo flight five years earlier, but on discovering that petrol was dripping down the back of her neck and that the gauge was broken she felt she might not have enough fuel to take her to France. (University of Ulster)

Amelia Earhart at the door of Robert Gallagher's house. She had just flown 2,026 miles in a little over thirteen hours from Harbor Grace in Newfoundland to land in one of his fields. (Bigger-McDonald Collection)

Amelia Earhart at the door of the house of Dan McCallion, the first man she spoke to on landing in Ireland according to her biographer, Doris Rich.

A sergeant and RUC constables guarding Earhart's plane. (Bigger-McDonald Collection)

The tailplane of *Friendship*, Amelia Earhart's bright red plane, which suffered somewhat at the hands of souvenir hunters. The plane is now in the Smithsonian Museum in Washington DC. (Bigger-McDonald Collection)

Sunday school outing by the Faughan river. (Bigger-McDonald Collection)

Part of the carnival procession in 1954 on its way along Rossville Street towards the Showgrounds, where the usual attractions were to be found. The letters DCBF stood for Derry Catholic Building Fund, a means of raising money to help build new churches and schools for the city parishes of Templemore and Clondermot. (University of Ulster)

The hiring-fair, or 'rabble', as it was called, in the west corner of the Diamond *c.*1930. They were held twice a year, in May and November, on three consecutive Wednesdays. The first Wednesday was 'release' day, when the hirelings of the previous semester could spend a week at home with their families (usually in Donegal). The second Wednesday was the hiring-fair proper, when new servants would be hired and new masters found. The third rabble was intended as a catch-up for farmers and clients who had not been suited the week before. The practice was discontinued by the mid-1930s. (Bigger-McDonald Collection)

The remains of a bicycle shop in John Street after a fire some time before 1910. The crowd of sightseers includes college boys with quasi-Eton collars and barefoot street urchins. The shop seems to have been a main dealer for Humber cycles. (University of Ulster)

6
Earning their Bread

Derry went from being one of the most prosperous of Irish cities in the nineteenth century to being one of the most depressed in the twentieth. The main cause was the coming of the Northern Ireland state and the Partition that cut off its natural hinterland, Donegal, Leitrim and Sligo. The effect was intensified by Stormont economic policy. The territory west of the Bann was not as politically reliable as that of east Ulster. Coleraine and north County Derry were steadfast enough, but the city could not be trusted and whatever little investment in job creation the pre-war province could afford, little found its way to the north-west. The shipyard closed and the busy port became less busy because of the stringently applied customs regulations. The result meant there was less work for the male population. What saved the city from the direst of economic straits was the shirt industry, which employed mainly women, and it was they who brought home the steady wage packet that kept the children fed. The situation produced a female workforce that was hard-working, independent and vocal. Catholic and Protestant workers laboured happily together except on occasions of seasonal tension, though the demography of the city meant that Catholics were in a majority. The effect on the unemployed men is one of the most interesting psychological studies that was never actually carried out. Derry still had its bakeries, its pork stores (in those years of high specification) and its working docks, but it also had large dole queues and the resultant depression and emigration. It was not until the coming of the Second World War that men, unemployed for years, found work in the necessary building associated with Derry the naval base, Derry the transit depot, and Derry the site of the anti-submarine school.

The cutting-room in the Star factory, Foyle Road, c.1929, showing Neil McMahon and John Donaghy. (Anna McMahon)

The staff of the Star factory, Foyle Road, *c.*1938. The factory, an elegant building, was built by Boyer & Co. to the design of Daniel Conroy in 1899. With the collapse of the shirt industry in the city it remained derelict for some years, a prey to vandals and arsonists, but is now restored as a riverside apartment building. (Courtesy Central Library, Derry)

Workers from McIntyre, Hogg and Marsh's City Factory supplementing their water supply from the Madden Mineral Waters Company that had its own private spring. The city's water supplies were greatly improved with the opening of Banagher Reservoir on 19 November 1935. (Bigger-McDonald Collection)

The yearly sale of Clydesdale horses bred by John C. Drennan at Carse Hall, near Limavady. (Bigger-McDonald Collection)

Pigs being rounded up for shipment on the hoof to Heysham at Queen's Quay. There used to be a passenger service but it was suspended in 1930. The cargo ships ceased to ply in 1963. (Bigger-McDonald Collection)

North-west Agricultural Society Show in the Showgrounds at the Brandywell enclosure. The building was custom–built with a 'Belfast' roof. (Bigger-McDonald Collection)

A meal break during hay-making at Bolies, a glen between Prehen Road and Strabane Old Road. (Anthony Crowe)

A typical turn-of-the-century pub with the rather uncompromising owners blocking the door. (Courtesy of University of Ulster)

Some of the management and staff of McColgan's, a large hardware and fancy goods store in Bishop Street Within (the walled city). (University of Ulster)

The staff of Edmiston & Co., a large hardware, jewellery and toy store in Shipquay Street. The founder of the firm, Wallace Edmiston, is the tall, hatted man in the centre of the picture. His son, Macrae Edmiston, is on the extreme right. The photograph was taken just before the staff's annual outing to Shrove, Co. Donegal, in the summer of 1939. (Bigger-McDonald Collection)

A gents' hairdressing saloon in Carlisle Road in 1922. The man on the extreme left of the picture is Dan Mailey. (Eddie Mailey)

The grocery and dry goods shop of Robert Elder, Duke Street, in 1912. Elder, pictured outside, worked as a salesman for the wholesaler's R. C. Malseed, but left to set up his own business on the river side of Duke Street. The shop was still there in the 1930s. The conspicuous barrel to the left would have contained salt herring, a staple of the time. (University of Ulster)

An unidentified fish-curing store pre-First World War. (University of Ulster)

A 1920s newsagent, rather grandiosely named. (Central Library, Derry)

Friel's grocer shop in Rossville Street and the corner of Union Street. (Harbour Museum; Derry City Council)

A second-hand clothing store on Waterloo Street opposite Butcher Gate *c*.1940. The Walker Pillar celebrating the hero of the siege can be seen through the mist. It was erected in 1826 on a site overlooking the Catholic Bogside and served as a significant icon for commemorations of the siege. It was blown up in 1973. (Charles Logue)

The art-deco frontage *c*.1935 of Romain Willman's hairdresser's. An immigrant from Alsace-Lorraine in the 1920s, he was the father of the actor, Noel Willman (1918–88). (Bigger-McDonald Collection)

The staff of Willman's hairdresser's neatly arranged about the proprietor, Romain Willman, who can be seen in the centre at the back. (Bigger-McDonald Collection)

A group of firemen photographed on the quay outside their new station in Fletcher Avenue, opposite Aberfoyle Terrace, in the 1920s. (Bigger-McDonald Collection)

A group of firemen complete with hose (1900s). In those years the fire station was in Hawkin Street. (Central Library, Derry)

The board of directors of the Londonderry Gaslight Company, 1877. The manager, Mr McNee, is standing to the right of the chairman, William McCarter. (Bigger-McDonald Collection)

The store of McCutcheon's shoe shop in Butcher Street in the early 1920s. (Bigger-McDonald Collection)

Bakers in Brewster's in Little James Street in the 1930s. The 'Important Notice' on the wall reminded workers that smoking on the premises meant dismissal. (Bigger-McDonald Collection)

A poultry stall outside St Columb's Hall in Newmarket Street which was showing the Chaplin film, *The Circus*, made in 1928. Street vending of food with minimal hygiene was a regular feature of Derry life. St Columb's Hall was built as a temperance establishment in 1888. Though its elaborately curved balcony meant that at least a third of the audience were looking across at each other, it served as a cinema and concert hall for many years. (Bigger-McDonald Collection)

The delivery cart of Bigger's pork store. The company was founded in 1844 by W. F. Bigger. A descendant also called W. F. Bigger was managing director when it was sold in 1952. (Bigger-McDonald Collection)

A man petting a donkey outside the Harbour Commissioners' building. It is thought he may have been a USPCA inspector. (Bigger-McDonald Collection)

Brewster's bread van at the Showgrounds, Brandywell (1929). The drivers were uncle and nephew. Bill Coyle (1914–90), the boy on the left, continued to work as a breadserver for all of his working life. The other man was Willie John McDaid. Both were from Rosemount. (Bernadette Barr)

A protest by the blind and partially sighted, some war casualties, passing lower Creggan Road *c.*1938. Their workshop was in the Gwyn's Institute in Brooke Park. In those days of minimal social services, their working conditions were severe. The basement where their workshops were located had stone floors and was generally unheated. (Anthony Crowe)

7
Playing the Game

D erry, like any Irish town worth the name, had its fair share of sporting activities. The usual games were played: soccer, rugby, cricket, hockey and bowling. Catholic schools had introduced Gaelic football and camogie, but they never gained the hold in the city that they had in other parts, especially in the south of the county. Gaelic football had been greeted with the same enthusiasm in Derry as elsewhere in the country after the foundation of the Gaelic Athletic Association in 1884, but its close association with Fenianism from its inception made it suspect in the eyes of the local clergy. They 'persuaded' local sportsmen to play soccer instead and their influence, not to say control, led to the establishment in the 1890s of a professional soccer team, Derry Celtic. Since then, though there has remained a limited local interest in Gaelic games the city has, on the whole, stayed dedicated to soccer. The local team, Derry City, has its ground at Brandywell, just under the hill that holds the city's cemetery. (This meant that it was customary before the Troubles for at least one uniformed RUC constable to take up his position in the cemetery to make sure that there were no rogue spectators.) Derry City was an important participant in the Irish Football Association's league and cup games and won the championship on a number of occasions. As the Northern Ireland Troubles grew darker and football matches became a cover for sectarian outrage Derry City withdrew from the IFA. (Now it is a significant member of the Football Association of Ireland, happy to travel the 300 miles to Cork fixtures.) One odd aspect of Derry sports life is the comparatively little use made of the river, an obvious amenity. It was not always so; the City of Derry Rowing Club was founded in 1860 and its memory was retained in the street name, Boating House Lane. Boating succumbed to the general malaise in the post-partition city; wartime restrictions and the security booms of the later Troubles tended to inhibit any attempt at a revival of the aquatic sport. Now, with a fine new clubhouse, the river will come into its own again.

A member of the City of Derry Rowing Club (founded in 1860), thought to be called Cunningham, photographed with an appropriate studio backdrop. The star on the oar blade is an indication of membership of the club.

A section of the crowd at Brandywell, the Derry City football grounds, c.1938. On the extreme left of the photograph, seated, is the well-known Derry character, Eddie 'Hawker' Lynch, who had the franchise for selling match programmes. (Bigger-McDonald Collection)

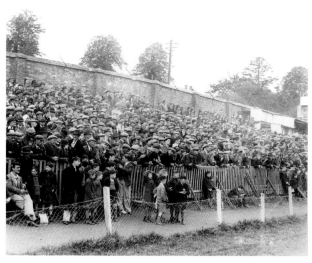

A bowler at the Duncreggan cricket ground in the early 1930s. The ground has since been redeveloped for housing. (Bigger-McDonald Collection)

Women's cricket in the early 1930s, perhaps slightly posed with the middle stump clearly hit and participants not in their complete gear. The match was played between Castlerock and Rossdowney LCC. The home team was defeated by the 'soccer' score of 9 runs to 15. (Bigger-McDonald Collection)

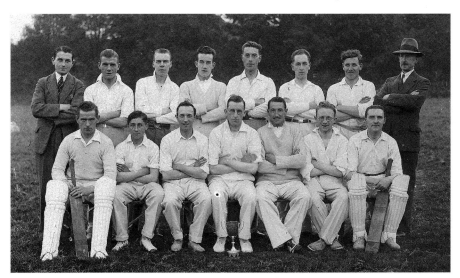

The champion YMCA cricket side with their minuscule trophy on the ground in front of the captain, George Stewart. The photograph was taken in the Aberfoyle cricket ground, Duncreggan Road, some time before 1932. (Bigger-McDonald Collection)

Michael Doherty of Chamberlain Street, billiards champion. The picture was taken in the recreation room of the Presbyterian Workingmen's Institute in the Diamond. Doherty was deaf and could not speak. (Bigger-McDonald Collection)

Soldiers playing hockey (a little half-heartedly). The peacetime army which felt it had to maintain a strong presence in Ebrington Barracks occupied its leisure time with appropriate pastimes, including cross-country runs, hunts and even polo. (Bigger-McDonald Collection)

William Goligher, a veteran of the First World War in which he lost a leg, in a pony and trap at Caw Brae. He was engaged in laying a trail for a garrison hunt. The younger man is a soldier, probably an officer from Ebrington Barracks. (Bigger-McDonald Collection)

A regatta at Prehen in the 1920s. The Star factory and the old Carlisle Bridge may be seen in the distance. (Harbour Museum; Derry City Council)

Competitors carrying skiffs down to the river at the Prehen regatta. (Harbour Museum; Derry City Council)

Bowling at Brooke Park in the early 1930s. (Bigger-McDonald Collection)

Children on the bowling green. (Bigger-McDonald Collection)

The Garrison hunt at Rossdowney, 1936 — a pastime for the peacetime army at leisure. (Bigger-McDonald Collection)

The Academical Institute Rugby XV, *c.*1890. The institute was built in 1870 by Matthew McClelland to the design of Richard Williamson, giving its name to Academy Road. It was intended for Presbyterians who had grown wary of certain Anglican tendencies they perceived in the curriculum of Foyle College. Fears were eventually allayed and the two schools were amalgamated in 1896. Bigger-McDonald Collection)

A Donegal-registered Ford car outside Phillip's in Shipquay Street with a notice saying, 'Last Lap'. The 1818 refers to the number of miles travelled by the car in seventy-two hours. The year was 1931. (Bigger-McDonald Collection)

The long jump at the Sports at Brandywell football grounds. (Bigger-McDonald Collection)

8
Trains and Boats and Planes

D erry in the heyday of the railway had four stations, two on each bank of the river. The London Midland and Scottish Company, which had Euston as its main metropolitan station, early established a Northern Counties Committee. The LMS(NCC) track went from its Waterside station on the east bank to Coleraine and thence to Belfast, providing the quickest means of reaching the short sea-route cross-channel steamers of Larne as well as those of the Belfast–Heysham and Belfast–Liverpool routes. It also branched off at Coleraine to the popular seaside resorts of Downhill, Castlerock, Portstewart and Portrush. The narrow-gauge County Donegal Railway (CDR) headed south and then west as far as Ballyshannon. On the west bank was the Londonderry and Lough Swilly Railway (L&LSR), which went north to Carndonagh via Buncrana and west to Burtonport via Letterkenny. Finally, there was the Great Northern Railway (GNR) that went to Belfast via Omagh, with the possibility of changing on to the Belfast–Dublin train at Portadown. These termini, owned by four different companies, were linked by a double-gauged track that ran under the Carlisle Bridge, which had replaced the old wooden structure in 1863. It in turn was demolished in 1932 to make room for the larger and wider Craigavon Bridge which was officially opened in March 1933. The city quays used to provide passenger services to Heysham in Lancashire and to Glasgow. The latter service, well known to the itinerant workers from Donegal, continued in operation into the early 1960s. The Foyle River is deep and wide, and therefore an appropriate venue for the 'summer cruise' of RAF seaplanes which were such a feature of life in the city in the early 1930s. Their coming was to be a foretaste of the city's importance during the Second World War. Derry, an important emigration port throughout the nineteenth century, was still the scene of sorrowful departures in these years. The transatlantic liners used to lie off Moville to receive passengers brought from the city in paddle-driven tenders.

James Gallivan, a merchant naval officer, in full dress uniform *c.*1899. (Bigger-McDonald Collection)

The Londonderry & Lough Swilly train on its way to Buncrana, passing the North West golf links at Lisfannon. The line, opened in 1863, was later extended to Buncrana, Ballyliffin and Carndonagh to the north, and through Letterkenny to Burtonport on the west coast of Donegal. Buses had replaced the train to Buncrana by 1935, but it was restored during the Second World War and continued to run until 1949. (Bigger-McDonald Collection)

An inspection of the permanent way of the Great Northern Railway on its approach to Derry in the early 1930s. The Carlisle Bridge, demolished in 1932, can be seen in the distance. (Bigger-McDonald Collection)

A steam yacht sailing downstream. St Columba's Church and the Waterside school may be seen between the masts. (Bigger-McDonald Collection)

PS *Seamore*, the Anchor Line tender which carried transatlantic passengers to Moville. The larboard paddle can be seen. The *Seamore*, which also served as a pleasure boat, was in service in Derry from 1928 to 1939 when the transatlantic liners ceased to call at Moville. (Bigger-McDonald Collection)

The SS *Lairdsburn* which occasionally complemented the *Lairdsloch* on the Derry–Glasgow route. The Burns Laird vessels, which had carried many holiday-makers in both directions in the summer, were also used by the itinerant Donegal workers, the 'tattie-hokers'. The ships, which in the days before stabilisers tended to roll badly in the choppy waters beyond Inishowen Head, ceased to travel on the route in 1966. (Bigger-McDonald Collection)

Women emigrants in the 1930s on the tender which would take them to board one of the transatlantic liners that regularly called at Moville. (Bigger-McDonald Collection)

A diver and support group during the building of Craigavon Bridge, September 1930. (Central Library, Derry)

The frontage of Lewis's travel agency in the early 1930s offering assisted passages to Australia and other parts of the empire. (Bigger-McDonald Collection)

The seaplane, Supermarine Southampton 1042, photographed on the Foyle opposite Princess Quay on 16 September 1931. The planes came on a yearly training exercise and landed in the Foyle on what they called their 'summer cruise'. (Bigger-McDonald Collection)

Supermarine Southampton 1042 landing in the Foyle watched by two men in the ferry boat, with Ebrington Barracks in the background. (Bigger-McDonald Collection)

Penny-farthing cyclists in 1885, members of the Londonderry Bicycle Club. The name came from the different sizes of the wheels. (The penny and the farthing were then the largest and the smallest copper coins.) The bicycle was propelled by pedals attached to the large front wheel. The machines were originally known as 'ordinaries', but the more fanciful name was irresistible. Coincidentally, that same year the first bicycle with a sprocket drive and chain and equal-sized wheels was invented. The taller of the two men is William Croom who invented the electric shirt-cutting band knife. (Bigger-McDonald Collection)

Two women with 'safety' cycles, as the new bicycles with equal-sized wheels were called. The photograph was taken *c.*1894. (Bigger-McDonald Collection)

A section of the old Carlisle Bridge being taken away on barges, early 1930s. The bridge, made of steel, had replaced the old wooden structure in 1863. Tolls were payable and the centre section was capable of swinging on a large pivot. (Bigger-McDonald Collection)

A notice concerning speed restrictions to be observed by heavy traffic on the Carlisle Bridge in 1932 prior to its demolition. (Bigger-McDonald Collection)

Craigavon Bridge, March 1933. The bridge was opened to pedestrians a few days before its official inauguration for full traffic. (Bigger-McDonald Collection)

The Rosemount bus on Infirmary Road passing the wall of the City and County Hospital and the top of Clarendon Street in the 1920s. The raised footpath was later removed. (Bigger-McDonald Collection)

Leyland buses belonging to H. M. S. Catherwood outside the Guildhall. Catherwood's red buses took over from the Corporation-run Municipal Omnibus Service in the 1920s. Catherwood continued to provide the service in the city and centralised the system of road transport for Northern Ireland as a whole. (Bigger-McDonald Collection)

Nurses at City and County Hospital with an ambulance belonging to St John's Brigade. The St John's Ambulance Association was established in 1877 as a voluntary service to provide first aid and emergency treatment at public events. It has been known as the St John's Ambulance since 1968. (Bigger-McDonald Collection)

A delivery van outside Copeland's grocery shop in Strand Road in the early 1930s. (Bigger-McDonald Collection)

A vintage Daimler outside R. R. A. Floyd's music store in Pump Street in an early advertising campaign (1905). The owner standing glumly in his doorway was known by the nickname, 'B-flat'. (Bigger-McDonald Collection)

9
Polls Apart

Derry, now notoriously known as Stroke City, has always had a troubled political history. The Stroke City appellation, an invention of the broadcaster, Gerry Anderson, to prevent the tedium of the continued use of Derry(stroke)Londonderry, arose from the vexed question of the city's name. The official name Londonderry, unacceptable to the nationalist majority, was rarely used even by unionists except to make a political point. By 1891 the Catholic population outnumbered Protestants by 4,500, but they did not gain control of the city until after Civil Rights agitation in the 1970s. There was a brief period of nationalist control (1920–23) when under the PR system a Catholic was elected mayor. Any hope of a repeat of this anomaly was dashed when the Northern Ireland Government abolished PR in 1922. From then until the City Corporation was dissolved in 1968 the minority unionists maintained a permanent majority of twelve to eight by a system of gerrymandering. It became extremely difficult for a Catholic to buy a house in the unionist-dominated North Ward. When the corporation began a belated housing scheme after the Second World War, care was taken that Catholics were, with rare exceptions, kept to the South Ward. In spite of this continuing affront to normal democratic practice, there was remarkably little rancour and the triumphalist elements of the Apprentice Boys' celebration of the closing of the city gates in 1688 were largely ignored. The 12 August normally meant decorative arches, bright banners and some very good marching bands. It wasn't until the Troubles grew darker that the sectarian underlay to the folksy fabric began to be manipulated for divisive ends. Now with general agreement there are the beginnings of a mutual respect for different traditions and cultures. The present arrangement of appointing mayors on a rota system, irrespective of party, has made the city an example of practical power-sharing.

Declaration of the election result for the Londonderry City constituency on the steps of the courthouse in Bishop Street Within. The by-election was occasioned by the death of the Duke of Abercorn in 1913. Davy Hogg, a Protestant shirt factory owner, stood as a Nationalist against the Conservative-Unionist candidate, Col. Pakenham. Strongly supported by Catholic voters, the local clergy and some liberal Protestants, Hogg defeated Pakenham by 2,699 votes to 2,642. (Harbour Museum; Derry City Council)

Members of the staff of Derry jail. The original building, designed by Edward Millar, dates from 1791. It was extended between 1819 and 1824. Now only one crenellated tower remains, marking the edge of an inner city housing estate. (Harbour Museum; Derry City Council)

A UVF battalion in Aubrey Street c.1915. The Ulster Volunteer Force was established in January 1913 as a means of defence against the imposition of Home Rule. Led by former British army officers and armed from Germany through Larne gun-running (24–25 April 1914), they were a formidable force. The group shown here are members of the 2nd Battalion City of Derry Regiment. (Bigger-McDonald Collection)

A group of B Specials training at Hawkin Street. The B men, as they were called, were the second and longest lasting category of special constabularies recruited in November 1920 to deal with the unrest following the establishment of the Northern Ireland state. Many were former members of the UVF and they continued to be used after the other

categories were stood down. They acted as a back-up for the RUC in 1926, were mobilised annually during the marching season, and served as a Home Guard during the Second World War and on border patrols during the IRA campaign of 1956–62. They were disbanded in 1970.

Sir Basil McFarland and members of the Londonderry Corporation on the occasion of his appointment as mayor of the city in May 1939. On his right is Patrick Maxwell, who led the Anti-Partitionist opposition in the council. On the left is Sir James Wilton, who served in the office from 1935 to 1939. At the back to the left is Councillor James McGeehan, an anti-partitionist who was heavily involved in amateur drama in the city. McFarland served for only five months before the war took him off to Egypt.

Apprentice Boys marching through Ferryquay Gate as part of the Siege commemoration on 12 August. The parade is led by the governor of the Apprentice Boys of Derry, Matthew Kerr, who had a printing business in London Street. On his right is the lieutenant-governor, Alex Birney, who, because he worked in a local bakery, was universally known as 'Cookie Bun'. (Bigger-McDonald Collection)

A meeting in the Corporation council chamber of the Honourable, the Irish Society, with the mayor, James Wilton, in the chair. The society had been founded in London in January 1610 by the merchant companies of the City of London. They had been heavily persuaded by James I to assume responsibility for the plantation of the city of Derry and Coleraine County. The vexed problem of the city's name, with its alien prefix, sprang from the society's establishment. (Bigger-McDonald Collection)

RUC officers at Victoria Barracks *c.*1930. (Bigger-McDonald Collection)

An Apprentice Boys' arch in Wapping Lane in the 1940s. The brotherhood, which has members in Ulster, Britain and Canada, holds marches each year around 18 December and 12 August to celebrate the shutting of the gates and the relief of the city that marked the end of the siege. New members must be initiated within the circle of the Derry Walls and, unlike the pattern of the Orange Order to which many belong, collarettes and other insignia are coloured 'Derry crimson' in memory of the bloody flag that flew during the siege. (Bigger-McDonald Collection)

An Apprentice Boys' arch at the foot of Cuthbert Street, Waterside. The band is the Hamilton. The panoply of the Boys' siege commemorations was just as elaborate as that of the anniversary of the Boyne held mainly in Belfast and the eastern counties a month earlier, though there were differences. The Apprentice Boys of Derry was founded in 1814 and named after the thirteen London apprentices who symbolically shut the gates of Derry against the Jacobite troops of Lord Antrim in December 1688. (Bigger-McDonald Collection)

The opening of the extension in 1937 to the Memorial Hall in Society Street. It was originally built in the baronial style as the Apprentice Boys' Hall in 1873. The new building was rededicated in 1937 as a memorial to members of the society who died in the First World War. (Bigger-McDonald Collection)

The removal in 1927 of the statue known as the 'Black Man' from its position at the head of Shipquay Street *en route* to its new location in Brooke Park. Sir Robert Alexander Ferguson (1796–1860) represented the city from 1840 to 1860, but rarely spoke in parliament. (Bigger-McDonald Collection)

The visit to Derry of Éamon de Valera in July 1951. Prominent Derry nationalists Patrick Maxwell and Eddie McAteer may be seen flanking the car as it moves up Brandywell Road. (Bigger-McDonald Collection)

10
Wars and Rumours of War

Derry always had a military presence. Ebrington Barracks was built in 1815 in the Waterside, to some complaint, but even then it was felt instinctively to be the safer side of the river. The city was used to the comings and goings of troops: church parades, guards of honour and occasional concerts in the parks. In 1933 General Balbo's air flotilla stopped off in Derry on its way to the Chicago World Fair, to let the world see what a great leader Il Duce was. It was a gala occasion for the city but also a demonstration of potential military force. The time of Munich brought a large recruitment of Territorials, forming the 24th and 25th Heavy Anti-Aircraft Batteries, who became all-week soldiers in September 1939 and were shipped off to Egypt for the duration. Lough Swilly, which like Killary Harbour in Connemara had been a safe haven for Royal Navy ships in the First World War, was no longer available, having been handed back to Éire in 1938. So Derry was to become a significant player in the Battle of the Atlantic. The city became full of servicemen: army, navy and airforce; and after Pearl Harbor, Yanks! There weren't many GIs or marines, but the American corvettes and destroyers, which acted as escort vessels to the Atlantic convoys, landed in Derry and the crews got five days' liberty. The city was shaken out of its thirties torpor, and the presence of so many exotic characters, free with cigarettes and candy, made life for Derry children a lot more exciting than before. The first influx of civilian technicians with their cowboy hats and boots in the spring of 1942 was like 'the pictures' come to life, and Derry men had well-paid work for the first time in decades. This lasted just a few years, but the city was never the same again.

Bandmaster Hays of the 2nd Battalion, South Wales Borderers, talking to Mr Justice Brown at the opening of the Spring Assizes in March 1937. Also in the picture is Capt. Connolly McCausland of Dreenagh, the County High Sheriff, wearing the parade uniform of the Irish Guards. As is clear from the picture, the judge was a man of considerable size and it was found necessary to install a bath of commensurate dimensions in the judicial lodgings in Carlisle Terrace.

The Hibernian Bank at the corner of Castle Street and Shipquay Street, protected by barbed wire and sandbags during the UVF and IRA violence in the spring and summer of 1920 in the months before the Government of Ireland Act (December 1920) which established Partition. (University of Ulster)

Soldiers of the Leicester Regiment arriving for a tour of duty at Ebrington Barracks. (Bigger-McDonald Collection)

A recruiting drive *c.*1938 for the 'modern army' showing a heavily armoured car (a First World War Rolls-Royce) and two cheery members of the Tank Corps with their characteristic berets. (Central Library, Derry)

Farewells at the LMS NCC station. The soldiers are members of the Leicester Regiment which served several tours in the city. (Bigger-McDonald Collection)

Soldiers at march past in the main square of Ebrington Barracks on the occasion of the visit of the Duke of Gloucester on 15 May 1935. (Bigger-McDonald Collection)

Members of the 25th Heavy Anti-Aircraft Battery, formed from men of the Territorial Army (TA) in the city, marching along the Limavady Road on 4 November 1939 from their camp at Caw to the railway station to board the train for Larne *en route* to Egypt. They are led by Capt. Sir Basil McFarland, with Lt E. H. Babington behind and Sgt Macrea Edmiston on his right. (Bigger-McDonald Collection)

Assembly after Requiem Mass in 1932 in St Columba's Church, Waterside, at the funeral of Lt Col. Creagh of the 2nd Battalion, Leicester Regiment. A native of Kanturk, Co. Cork, he was stationed at Ebrington Barracks and died of a heart attack on Lisfannon links. (Bigger-McDonald Collection)

Two B Specials on guard at Galliagh customs post in November 1939. The car, towards which the hatless army officer is walking accompanied by a customs officer, has wartime covers on its headlights, permitting only slits of illumination.

Termon Street off Bonds Hill showing an air-raid shelter and across the river several naval corvettes. The shelters were crude brick structures strengthened with steel rods except for an escape hatch of brick. They were originally fitted with wooden lath doors, which tended to disappear at bonfire time. The city was fortunate in that they were never tested. (Richard Doherty)

A half-inflated barrage balloon and its truck in a field in Trench Road, Waterside, in 1940. The balloons were filled with hydrogen and flown on steel cables. They were intended as a deterrent against low-flying German aircraft and the skies around the city were filled with these strangely-eerie silver blimps during the early years of the Second World War. They were manned by RAF Balloon Command (920 Squadron). From 1944 the tarpaulin, no longer required for the balloons, was adapted for more domestic uses, like schoolbags and rainproof jackets. (University of Ulster)

One of the twenty-four flying-boats of General Count Italo Balbo's air flotilla which stopped in Derry in July 1933 *en route* to the Centennial Exhibition in Chicago. It was a twin-hulled Savoia Marchetti with a limited range, so that landing for refuelling before the Atlantic hop was necessary. The seaplanes landed in the Foyle, causing some excitement and curiosity in the city. (Bigger-McDonald Collection)

General Count Italo Balbo (1896–40), the Italian chargé d'affaires, and members of his *Regia Aeronautica* with members of the Italian community in Derry, including Victor Fiorentini in July 1933. Balbo was a strong supporter of Mussolini but disapproved of his association with Hitler. He became Secretary of State for Air in 1926. Appointed Governor of Libya in 1934, he was killed in 1940 when his plane was shot down by friendly fire from Italian anti-aircraft guns. (Bigger-McDonald Collection)

General Balbo, the Italian chargé d'affaires, Dudley McCorkell, the mayor, Sir Henry Millar, the town clerk, and other civic dignitaries on the steps of the Guildhall. (Bigger-McDonald Collection)

A section of a group of Italian fliers who accompanied General Balbo. (Bigger-McDonald Collection)

Derry children outside the Rialto Cinema in 1942. Each is holding a bag of candies supplied by the US Navy. The American forces were a constant source of sweets for Derry children and of cigarettes for their parents. Hershey bars, Baby Ruth and peanut brittle became part of the tooth-loosening diet for the children, while Lucky Strike, Camels and Philip Morris were even more deleterious to adult health. (Bigger-McDonald Collection)

A queue of sightseers waits to board a British destroyer, a relic of the First World War, on a Royal Navy open day in the 1930s. (Bigger-McDonald Collection)

A US sailor, unable to believe his eyes at a tourist postcard coming true, drives a donkey cart at Cross Street, Rosemount, in 1943. (Richard Doherty)

Three US sailors outside Littlewood's store in Waterloo Place, wearing the blue heavy-weather gear that they swore was needed only in Derry. The naval personnel who came to Derry were usually members of the crews of destroyers, which acted as escort vessels for North Atlantic convoys (1942-44). They usually had a five-day turn-around. (Richard Doherty)

A party of women laying wreaths on a very wet day at the War Memorial in the Diamond. Since there were no men present, it must have been on some occasion other than Remembrance Day. The memorial, designed by Vernon March, was officially opened on 23 June 1927 by Maj.-Gen. F. F. Ready. (Bigger-McDonald Collection)